W9-CNZ-490

LES PETITS PLATS
FRANÇAIS
SIMON & SCHUSTER
ILLUSTRATED

fantastic flans and tarts

CATHERINE KLUGER

Photography by Olivier Malingue
Styling by Élodie Rambaud

LIBRARY
NSCC, AKERLEY CAMPUS
21 WOODLAWN RD.
DARTMOUTH, NS B2W 2R7 CANADA

SIMON &
SCHUSTER
ILLUSTRATED

London · New York · Sydney · Toronto
A CBS COMPANY

English language edition published in Great Britain by
Simon and Schuster UK Ltd, 2011
A CBS Company

Copyright © Marabout 2010

SIMON AND SCHUSTER
ILLUSTRATED BOOKS
Simon & Schuster UK
222 Gray's Inn Road
London WC1X 8HB
www.simonandschuster.co.uk

This book is copyright under the Berne Convention.
No reproduction without permission.
All rights reserved.

The right of Catherine Kluger to be identified as the Author of this Work has
been asserted by her in accordance with sections 77 and 78 of the Copyright,
Designs and Patents Act, 1988.

1 2 3 4 5 6 7 8 9 10

Translation: Prudence Ivey
Copy editor English language: Nicki Lampon

Colour reproduction by Dot Gradations Ltd, UK
Printed and bound in U.A.E.

ISBN 978-0-85720-358-8

Contents

How to use this book

Almost all of the tarts in this book use precooked savoury or sweet pastry cases. To make your own, refer to the basic pastry recipes on the next few pages. Many of the savoury tarts also use a basic quiche filling, which is provided here.

Can I reheat these tarts?

Do not use a microwave oven to cook or reheat tarts; the pastry will soften and the texture will become soggy. It is far better to reheat for 5 minutes – and to cook from scratch – in a traditional oven.

Can I freeze these tarts?

All these recipes should be eaten fresh. You should not freeze a tart as it will lose its flavours and become watery.

Basic quiche filling

Preparation time: 3 minutes

3 eggs
200 ml (7 fl oz) milk
65 ml (2¼ fl oz) double cream
salt and freshly ground black pepper

Mix the eggs, milk, cream and a little seasoning together and beat vigorously.

Shortcrust pastry

Preparation time: 20 minutes +
1 ½ hours chilling
Cooking time: 30 minutes

200 g (7 oz) plain flour, sifted
a pinch of salt
90 g (3 oz) very cold butter, cubed
1 egg, beaten
20 ml (¾ fl oz) iced water

Mix the flour and salt together in a bowl then add the butter. Rub in with your fingertips until you have a breadcrumb-like consistency without warming the butter too much.

Add the egg and then the cold water, working as little as possible, ideally with the flat of your hands, to knead the mixture to a smooth paste. You can also make the pastry in a food processor, if you wish.

Wrap the pastry in cling film and chill in the fridge for at least 1 hour. When you remove from the fridge, flatten the pastry by banging on a flat surface.

Flour a clean dry work surface and roll out the pastry until slightly larger than your tart dish. Prick lightly with a fork. Grease the tart dish or mould then lay the pastry over the dish and press it into the base and sides. Chill for at least 30 minutes.

Preheat the oven to 160°C (fan oven 140°C), Gas Mark 3.

Cut out a disc of baking parchment the same size and shape as the tin and put in the base of the tart. Add baking beans and bake for around 30 minutes (this is called baking blind).

Remove the paper and baking beans and brush the pastry with a little beaten egg. Return to the oven for a further 3 minutes before using.

Tip: You must use very cold butter and chill the pastry before rolling out. It should also be chilled before baking or it will puff up or shrink back.

Variations: Add a pinch of poppy seeds, white or black sesame seeds, cumin seeds or caraway seeds when mixing the flour and salt together.

Sweet pastry

Preparation time: 20 minutes +
1½ hours chilling
Cooking time: 30 minutes

200 g (7 oz) plain flour, sifted
25 g (1 oz) ground almonds
80 g (2¾ oz) icing sugar
a pinch of salt
120 g (4¼ oz) very cold butter,
cubed
1 egg, beaten

Mix the flour, ground almonds, icing sugar and salt together then add the butter. Rub in with your fingertips until you have a breadcrumb-like consistency without warming the butter too much.

Add the egg, working as little as possible, ideally with the flat of your hands, to knead the mixture to a smooth paste. You can also make the pastry in a food processor, if you wish.

Wrap the pastry in cling film and chill in the fridge for at least 1 hour. When you remove from the fridge, flatten the pastry by banging on a flat surface.

Flour a clean dry work surface and roll out the pastry to slightly larger than your tart dish. Prick lightly with a fork. Grease the tart dish or mould then lay the pastry over the dish and press it into the base and sides. Chill for at least 30 minutes.

Preheat the oven to 160°C (fan oven 140°C), Gas Mark 3. Cook the pastry base for 20 minutes (this is called baking blind). Leave to cool before using.

Tip: You must use very cold butter and chill the pastry before rolling out. It should also be chilled before baking otherwise it will puff up or shrink back.

Variations: Replace the ground almonds with ground hazelnuts or pistachios, or add some vanilla seeds, cinnamon or cocoa powder.

Tuna, pea and mint quiche

Preparation time: 20 minutes
Cooking time: 30 minutes
Serves 6

100 g (3½ oz) peas (fresh or frozen)
salt
1 tablespoon Dijon mustard
50 g (1¾ oz) grated Parmesan
  cheese
3 fresh mint sprigs, finely chopped
1 quantity basic quiche filling (see
  page 4)
1 shortcrust pastry case (see
  page 6), baked blind
185 g can tuna in spring water,
  drained

Preheat the oven to 160°C (fan oven 140°C), Gas Mark 3.

Cook the peas in boiling salted water for 5 minutes. Drain and immediately plunge them into iced water so that they stop cooking and keep their green colour.

Mix together the mustard, Parmesan, mint and quiche filling.

Place half the peas in the pastry case, then add the tuna, followed by the remaining peas.

Pour the quiche mixture into the pastry case until it reaches the top then cook in the preheated oven for 30 minutes.

Carrot, pickled lemon and coriander quiche

Preparation time: 30 minutes +
1 hour resting
Cooking time: 30 minutes
Serves 6

200 g (7 oz) carrots, peeled
sea salt
1 shortcrust pastry case (see
page 6), baked blind
50 g (1¾ oz) pickled lemons, rinsed,
dried and finely chopped
½ bunch of fresh coriander, finely
chopped
1 quantity basic quiche filling
(see page 4)

Cut the carrots into very fine ribbons using a vegetable peeler or kitchen mandolin. Cover in sea salt and leave for at least 1 hour, then carefully brush off the salt with kitchen towel.

Preheat the oven to 160°C (fan oven 140°C), Gas Mark 3.

Place the carrot strips in the pastry case, resting them on their edges as vertical as possible to add volume to the filling.

Add the pickled lemons to the carrots and sprinkle with the coriander. Pour the quiche mixture into the case until it reaches the top and cook for 30 minutes.

Tomato, courgette, mozzarella and basil quiche

Preparation time: 40 minutes
Cooking time: 35 minutes
Serves 6

6 tablespoons olive oil
150 g (5¼ oz) courgettes, finely
    sliced
1 garlic clove, finely chopped
1 onion, finely chopped
300 g (10½ oz) fresh tomatoes,
    half peeled, de-seeded and finely
    chopped and half finely sliced
a small bunch of fresh basil,
    chopped
1 shortcrust pastry case (see
    page 6), baked blind
100 g (3½ oz) mozzarella, finely
    sliced
1 quantity basic quiche filling
    (see page 4)

Preheat the oven to 160°C (fan oven 140°C), Gas Mark 3.

Heat half the oil in a frying pan and fry the courgettes over a high heat. Set aside.

Heat the rest of the oil, add the garlic, onion and finely chopped tomatoes and leave to simmer for around 20 minutes.

Away from the heat, add the basil.

Spread the cooked tomato sauce over the bottom of the pastry case. Add a layer of courgette slices, arranged in a spiral, then alternate layers of mozzarella and tomato slices. Repeat the layers if necessary. Pour the quiche mixture into the pastry case until it reaches the top and cook for 35 minutes.

Tip: Serve hot before the mozzarella cools and sets.

Variation: You can replace the basil with about 10 g (¼ oz) of marjoram if you wish.

Crab, sorrel and spinach quiche

Preparation time: 20 minutes
Cooking time: 30 minutes
Serves 6

100 g (3½ oz) crab meat (canned
  or frozen), drained if necessary
  and flaked
150 g (5¼ oz) spinach, washed
a bunch of sorrel leaves, washed
1 shortcrust pastry case (see
  page 6), baked blind
1 quantity basic quiche filling
  (see page 4)

Preheat the oven to 160°C (fan oven
140°C), Gas Mark 3.

Blot the crab meat dry with kitchen
towel (if it is too wet the quiche will
be soggy).

Wilt the spinach and sorrel in
separate pans with a little boiling
salted water. Drain separately, blot
dry and chop.

Spread the chopped spinach over
the bottom of the pastry case and
top with the crab meat. Sprinkle with
the chopped sorrel. Pour the quiche
mixture into the pastry case until
it reaches the top and cook for
30 minutes. Serve hot.

Ham, crispy bacon and Parmesan tart

Preparation time: 20 minutes
Cooking time: 10 minutes
Serves 6

1 shortcrust pastry case (see page 6), baked blind

Filling
20 g (¾ oz) smoked bacon
25 g (1 oz) Parmesan cheese, finely sliced
150 g (5¼ oz) sliced ham
50 g (1¾ oz) Prosciutto slices

Béchamel sauce
35 g (1¼ oz) butter
35 g (1¼ oz) flour
350 ml (12 fl oz) milk
50 g (1¾ oz) Gruyère cheese, grated
salt and freshly ground black pepper

Preheat the oven to 170°C (fan oven 150°C), Gas Mark 3½.

Grill the bacon until crispy then place the Parmesan slices under the grill until melted. Leave to cool to form Parmesan crisps.

Prepare the béchamel sauce: heat the butter in a small pan, add the flour and beat to make a roux. Slowly add the milk.

Once the mixture has thickened, remove from the heat, add the Gruyère and season. Leave to cool then mix in 1 finely chopped slice of ham.

Half fill the prepared pastry case with the béchamel mixture.

Cut the remaining slices of ham and Prosciutto into three and roll each piece into a cone around your finger. Place in the béchamel mixture and finish with the grilled bacon and Parmesan crisps.

Cook for around 10 minutes and serve immediately.

Tip: This tart can be prepared in advance and kept in the fridge but it must only be cooked just before serving.

Variation: Decorate with coriander or flat leaf parsley browned in oil.

Salmon, leek and mushroom quiche

Preparation time: 20 minutes
Cooking time: 30 minutes
Serves 6

4 tablespoons olive oil
200 g (8¾ oz) leeks, finely chopped
150 g (5¼ oz) mushrooms, finely
  sliced
250 g (8¾ oz) salmon fillet
a small bunch of fresh dill, chopped
1 shortcrust pastry case (see
  page 6), baked blind
1 quantity basic quiche filling (see
  page 4)
1 tablespoon pink peppercorns,
  crushed

Preheat the oven to 160°C (fan oven
140°C), Gas Mark 3.

Heat 2 tablespoons of the oil in a pan
and fry the leeks with a little water
for 10 minutes. Remove to a bowl.

Heat the remaining 2 tablespoons
of oil and fry the mushrooms.

Meanwhile, steam the salmon for
10 minutes or until cooked. Break into
flakes, being sure to remove
any skin and bones. Mix the salmon
with the leeks, mushrooms and
chopped dill.

Spread the mixture over the base
of the pastry case. Pour in the quiche
mixture to the top of the case,
sprinkle with the peppercorns and
cook for 30 minutes.

Spinach, ricotta and bresaola quiche

Preparation time: 40 minutes
Cooking time: 35 minutes
Serves 6

300 g (10½ oz) spinach, washed
a small bunch of fresh parsley,
   chopped
2 slices bresaola
1 shortcrust pastry case (see
   page 6), baked blind
150 g (5¼ oz) ricotta, drained
1 quantity basic quiche filling
   (see page 4)
15 g (½ oz) sesame seeds or
   pine nuts, toasted

Preheat the oven to 160°C (fan oven 140°C), Gas Mark 3.

Bring a pan of water to the boil and cook the spinach for a few seconds until wilted. Drain and press out as much liquid as possible.

Chop the cooked spinach and mix with the parsley and a roughly chopped slice of bresaola. Spread over the bottom of the pastry case.

Crumble the ricotta and mix with the quiche filling before pouring the mixture into the quiche case until it reaches the top. Finely chop the second slice of bresaola and sprinkle on top. Sprinkle over the sesame seeds or pine nuts and press gently into the surface of the quiche.

Cook for 35 minutes. Serve hot.

Variation: You can make an equally delicious vegetarian version of this tart by leaving out the bresaola.

Courgette and Feta quiche with Parmesan crumble

Preparation time: 40 minutes
Cooking time: 30 minutes
Serves 6

1 shortcrust pastry case (see page 6), baked blind
1 quantity basic quiche filling (see page 4)

Parmesan crumble
50 g (1¾ oz) butter
50 g (1¾ oz) plain flour
50 g (1¾ oz) grated Parmesan cheese

Filling
150 g (5¼ oz) courgettes
1 garlic clove, finely chopped
grated zest of 1 lemon
2 tablespoons olive oil
50 g (1¾ oz) Feta cheese, crumbled

Preheat the oven to 170°C (fan oven 150°C), Gas Mark 3½.

Prepare the crumble by rubbing the butter into the flour and Parmesan. Spread on to a baking tray covered with baking parchment and cook for 10 minutes.

Reduce the oven temperature to 160°C (fan oven 140°C), Gas Mark 3.

Meanwhile, wash the courgettes and grate with a large-holed grater. Leave to dry on kitchen towel.

Over a high heat, fry the garlic and lemon zest in the oil then add the courgettes and mix well.

Leave the courgettes to cool then mix with the Feta cheese. Spread over the bottom of the pastry case. Pour the quiche mixture into the pastry case until it reaches the top and cook for 30 minutes.

Remove the cooked tart from the oven, sprinkle generously with the Parmesan crumble and serve hot.

Mushroom, chive and chicken quiche

Preparation time: 30 minutes
Cooking time: 30 minutes
Serves 6

150 g (5¼ oz) chanterelle
  mushrooms, chopped
2 shallots, finely chopped
3 tablespoons olive oil
150 g (5¼ oz) chicken breast,
  cubed
1 teaspoon paprika
a bunch of fresh chives, finely
  chopped
1 shortcrust pastry case
  (see page 6), baked blind
1 quantity basic quiche filling
  (see page 4)

Preheat the oven to 160°C (fan oven 140°C), Gas Mark 3.

Heat a frying pan and fry the mushrooms and half the shallots in half the oil. Set aside in a bowl.

Fry the cubed chicken with the remaining shallots and oil and the paprika.

Mix the mushroom and chicken mixtures together with the chopped chives and spread all the ingredients over the bottom of the pastry case.

Pour in the quiche mixture to the top of the case and cook for 30 minutes. Serve hot.

Cod, fennel and sun-dried tomato quiche

Preparation time: 30 minutes +
30 minutes chilling
Cooking time: 30 minutes
Serves 6

50 g (1¾ oz) sun-dried tomatoes,
drained
30 g (1 oz) pitted black olives
1 garlic clove
200 g (7 oz) cod fillet, cubed
150 g (5¼ oz) fennel, finely chopped
2 tablespoons olive oil
1 shortcrust pastry case (see
page 6), baked blind
1 quantity basic quiche filling
(see page 4)

Blend together the tomatoes, olives
and garlic. Add to the fish and mix
gently to cover with the mixture.
Set aside in the fridge for at least
30 minutes.

Preheat the oven to 160°C (fan oven
140°C), Gas Mark 3.

Heat a frying pan and cook the fennel
in the olive oil and a little water over a
low heat. Set aside.

Using the same pan, fry the fish
mixture for 4 minutes, turning gently.

Spread the fennel over the bottom
of the pastry case then add the cod
on top. Pour the quiche mixture in so
it reaches the top of the pastry case
and cook for 30 minutes. Serve hot.

Grilled pepper pesto and goat's cheese quiche

Preparation time: 30 minutes + cooling
Cooking time: 35 minutes
Serves 6

400 g (14 oz) red peppers
50 g (1¾oz) almonds
grated zest of 1 lemon
1 garlic clove
a few fresh basil leaves
3 tablespoons olive oil
2 teaspoons balsamic vinegar
150 g (5¼ oz) goat's cheese, crumbled
1 shortcrust pastry case (see page 6), baked blind
1 quantity basic quiche filling (see page 4)
50 g (1¾ oz) Parmesan cheese

Preheat the oven to 200°C (fan oven 180°C), Gas Mark 6.

Place the peppers on a baking tray and cook in the oven for 25 minutes or until the skins are black, turning regularly. Remove from the oven and leave to cool.

Once the peppers are cool, peel and remove the seeds. Cut one pepper into strips.

Blend the remaining peppers with the almonds, lemon zest, garlic, basil, oil and balsamic vinegar until you have a very fine pesto.

Scatter the strips of pepper and crumbled goat's cheese over the base of the pastry case.

Mix the pepper pesto and quiche filling together. Pour into the pastry case right to the top then sprinkle with the Parmesan.

Cook for 35 minutes and serve hot.

Chicken, aubergine caponata and black olive quiche

Preparation time: 45 minutes +
12 hours marinating
Cooking time: 30 minutes
Serves 6

100 g (3½ oz) passata
2 tablespoons olive oil, plus
   extra for frying
150 g (5¼ oz) chicken breast,
   cut into strips
1 onion, finely chopped
1 celery stick, finely chopped
300 g (10½ oz) aubergine, diced
230 g can chopped tomatoes
35 g (1¼ oz) pitted black olives,
   chopped
20 g (¾ oz) capers
2 tablespoons balsamic vinegar
salt and freshly ground black pepper
1 shortcrust pastry case
   (see page 6), baked blind
1 quantity basic quiche filling
   (see page 4)

The day before you want to eat, mix together the passata and olive oil, add the chicken and leave to marinate in the fridge.

The next day, preheat the oven to 160°C (fan oven 140°C), Gas Mark 3.

Heat a frying pan and cook the onion and celery in a little oil. Add the aubergine to the pan and cook until starting to soften. Add the canned tomatoes, olives and capers.

Cook for 30 minutes then remove the capers, add the balsamic vinegar and leave to cook for another 5 minutes. Set aside.

Fry the chicken, season and mix with the aubergine caponata.

Pour this mixture over the bottom of the pastry case. Add the quiche mixture until it reaches the top of the case and cook for 30 minutes.

Bottarga, courgette and parsley quiche

Preparation time: 20 minutes
Cooking time: 30 minutes
Serves 6

200 g (7 oz) courgettes
25 g (1 oz) bottarga
1 shortcrust pastry case (see
  page 6), baked blind
a bunch of fresh flat leaf parsley,
  finely chopped
1 quantity basic quiche filling
  (see page 4)

Preheat the oven to 160°C (fan oven 140°C), Gas Mark 3.

Wash the courgettes, trim and slice into thin strips with a vegetable peeler or mandolin. Remove the wax covering the bottarga and grate the fish eggs with a large-holed grater.

Place the courgette strips into the pastry case, resting them on their edges as vertically as possible so as to retain volume. Add the parsley then the bottarga. Pour the quiche mixture into the case to the top and cook for 30 minutes. Serve hot.

Tip: Bottarga is the salted, pressed and dried roe of tuna or grey mullet. It is available from good Italian delis or online.

Roasted cherry tomato and rocket pesto tart

Preparation time: 20 minutes
Cooking time: 25–35 minutes
Serves 6

650 g (1 lb 5 oz) cherry tomatoes
sea salt
100 ml (3½ fl oz) olive oil, plus
 extra for the tomatoes
100 g (3½ oz) rocket
1 garlic clove
20 g (¾ oz) pine nuts
1 shortcrust pastry case (see
 page 6), baked blind
coarsely ground black pepper

Preheat the oven to 150°C (fan oven 130°C), Gas Mark 2.

Cut the tomatoes in half or leave whole if they are small. Place on a roasting tray. Add some salt to each tomato, drizzle with olive oil and cook for 25–35 minutes.

Blend the rocket with the olive oil, garlic and pine nuts until you have a very smooth pesto.

Place the tomatoes in the pastry case, removing any tomato stalks if wished. Pour over the pesto, add a little seasoning and serve immediately while hot.

Variation: Instead of the pesto, reduce 6 tablespoons of balsamic vinegar in a saucepan to get a syrup or use a balsamic glaze.

Three ham and mustard quiche

Preparation time: 25 minutes

Cooking time: 30 minutes
Serves 6

50 g (1¾ oz) bacon
50 g (1¾ oz) Parmesan cheese,
  finely sliced
2 slices cooked ham, chopped
2 slices dry-cured ham, chopped
1 shortcrust pastry case (see
  page 6), baked blind
1 tablespoon wholegrain mustard
1 quantity basic quiche filling
  (see page 4)

Preheat the oven to 160°C (fan oven 140°C), Gas Mark 3.

Heat the grill to medium and grill the bacon and slices of Parmesan.

Sprinkle the two hams and bacon over the bottom of the pastry case. Crumble the Parmesan on top.

Mix the mustard with the basic quiche filling. Pour the mixture into the pastry case until it reaches the top then cook for 30 minutes.

Scallop and leek quiche

Preparation time: 40 minutes
Cooking time: 30 minutes
Serves 6

1 tablespoon olive oil
150 g (5¼ oz) scallops with
  corals attached
150 g (5¼ oz) leeks, chopped
1 shortcrust pastry case (see
  page 6), baked blind
1 quantity basic quiche filling
  (see page 4)
½ a bunch of fresh dill

Preheat the oven to 160°C (fan oven 140°C), Gas Mark 3.

Heat the oil and quickly fry the scallops to brown them on each side without cooking through. Set aside.

Add the leeks to the pan with a little water and leave to cook gently for 5–10 minutes.

Place the leeks in the bottom of the pastry case, followed by the scallops.

Pour the quiche mixture to the top of the pastry case, scatter over the dill and cook for 30 minutes. Serve hot.

Variation: Add some truffle oil to the tart when taking it out of the oven, just before serving.

Chocolate apricot tart with chocolate crumble

Preparation time: 45 minutes
Cooking time: 30 minutes
Serves 8

50 g (1¾ oz) butter
200 g (7 oz) apricots, halved
  and stoned
50 g (1¾ oz) caster sugar
1 sweet pastry case (see
  pages 8–9), baked blind

Chocolate crumble
100 g (3½ oz) caster sugar
60 g (2 oz) ground almonds
120 g (4¼ oz) butter
80 g (2¾ oz) plain flour
20 g (¾ oz) cocoa powder

Filling
100 ml (3½ fl oz) double cream
1 egg
1 tablespoon plain flour
1 tablespoon caster sugar
1 tablespoon cocoa powder

Preheat the oven to 170°C (fan oven 150°C), Gas Mark 3½.

Prepare the crumble by rubbing all the ingredients together with your fingertips to get a crumb-like mixture. Spread on a baking tray and cook for 10 minutes. Remove from the oven and leave to cool.

Reduce the oven temperature to 160°C (fan oven 140°C), Gas Mark 3.

Melt the butter in a saucepan, add the apricots and sugar and heat until lightly caramelised.

Prepare the filling by whisking all the ingredients together in a bowl.

Arrange the apricots in the pastry case and pour in the flan mixture around them. Cook for 30 minutes.

Remove the tart from the oven and sprinkle with the crumble mixture before serving.

Passion fruit tart with hazel and coconut meringue

Preparation time: 30 minutes +
  12 hours chilling
Cooking time: 45 minutes
Serves 8

1 sweet pastry case (see
  pages 8–9), baked blind
grated zest of 1 lime

Passion fruit cream
100 g (3½ oz) caster sugar
4 eggs
125 g (4½ oz) ready-made passion
  fruit purée
grated zest of 1 lemon
125 g (4½ oz) butter

Hazel and coconut meringue
1 egg white
60 g (2 oz) caster sugar
15 g (½ oz) ground hazelnuts
15 g (½ oz) desiccated coconut

For the passion fruit cream, whisk together the sugar, eggs, passion fruit purée and lemon zest in a saucepan. Leave to thicken over a low heat, whisking constantly for 5–7 minutes. Pour the warm mixture over the butter and mix well until you have a smooth, glossy consistency. Leave to cool in the fridge for at least 12 hours.

For the meringue, preheat the oven to 160°C (fan oven 140°C), Gas Mark 3. Whisk the egg white to very firm peaks, add the sugar and continue to beat until glossy. Gently fold in the ground hazelnuts and coconut. Grease a baking tray or line it with baking parchment then pipe on the meringue in lines.

Reduce the oven heat to 110°C (fan oven 90°C), Gas Mark ¼. Cook for 45 minutes. The meringue should be dry and crisp. Leave to cool then crumble into pieces.

With a piping bag or spatula, spread the passion fruit cream into the prepared pastry case, smoothing the surface a little if necessary. Add the crumbled meringue around the edges of the tart then sprinkle the top with the lime zest.

Tip: This tart should be kept in the fridge and eaten cold. The meringue will keep separately for a few days in a metal container.

Cheesecake with ginger biscuit base

Preparation time: 45 minutes
Cooking time: 35–40 minutes
Serves 8

200 g (7 oz) ginger biscuits
50 g (1¾ oz) butter, melted
500 g (1 lb 2 oz) cream cheese
3 eggs
50 g (1¾ oz) crème fraîche
150 g (5¼ oz) caster sugar
2 teaspoons vanilla extract
grated zest of 1 lemon
grated zest of 1 lime
50 g (1¾ oz) plain flour

Preheat the oven to 160°C (fan oven 140°C), Gas Mark 3.

Crush the biscuits and mix with the melted butter. Press into the base of your cheesecake tin or dish with the flat of your hand. Cook in the oven for 25–30 minutes.

Increase the oven temperature to 170°C (fan oven 150°C), Gas Mark 3½.

Mix the cream cheese, eggs, crème fraîche, sugar, vanilla extract and lemon and lime zest together. Once smooth, add the flour and mix until all the lumps have gone. Pour over the cooked biscuit base.

Cook for 35–40 minutes. The cheesecake is cooked when it has turned a light golden colour.

Leave to cool before eating.

Summer berries with green tea cream and almond paste

Preparation time: 40 minutes +
12 hours chilling
Cooking time: 15 minutes
Serves 8

1 sweet pastry case (see
pages 8–9), baked blind
115 g (4 oz) almond paste
25 g (1 oz) honey
icing sugar, for dusting (optional)

Green tea cream
1 egg
1 egg yolk
1 tablespoon plain flour
250 ml (9 fl oz) milk
60 g (2 oz) caster sugar
2 tablespoons green tea powder

Summer fruit
175 g (6¼ oz) strawberries
100 g (3½ oz) raspberries
50 g (1¾ oz) redcurrants
25 g (1 oz) blackberries
25 g (1 oz) blueberries

Preheat the oven to 160°C (fan oven 140°C), Gas Mark 3.

Cut the sides from the pastry case to create a disc, without removing from the tin or dish.

Roll the almond paste into a sausage. Place it around the edge of the tart and pinch with your fingers to make a dented pattern.

Cook for 15 minutes. The almond paste should not be overcooked as it will become too hard to eat.

For the green tea cream, beat the egg, egg yolk and flour together. Heat the milk and sugar then pour the warm mixture over the eggs and flour and whisk to a smooth, glossy cream. Add the green tea powder and chill in the fridge for at least 12 hours.

Spread the cream on to the tart base and decorate with the fruit.

With a fork, add little droplets of honey to the top of the tart. Dust the almond paste sides with icing sugar, if using. Serve cold.

Tip: The almond paste gives a chic edge to this tart. You could also make a simpler version without the almond paste.

TARTES
KLUGER
FABRIQUE DE TARTES

Coffee and chocolate tart

Preparation time: 20 minutes
Cooking time: 25 minutes
Serves 8

150 g (5¼ oz) dark chocolate,
  broken into pieces
3 eggs, separated
100 g (3½ oz) caster sugar
50 ml (2 fl oz) espresso coffee
75 g (2½ oz) butter, melted
25 g (1 oz) plain flour
1 teaspoon baking powder
a pinch of salt
1 sweet pastry case (see
  pages 8–9), baked blind

Preheat the oven to 160°C (fan oven 140°C), Gas Mark 3.

Melt the chocolate in bowl over a pan of simmering water.

Whisk the egg yolks with the sugar until they turn pale. Add the coffee and butter then the melted chocolate, flour and baking powder. Mix with a spatula.

Whisk the egg whites and salt to firm peaks and gently fold into the chocolate mixture.

Pour into the prepared pastry case and cook for 25 minutes.

Milk chocolate and hazelnut tart

Preparation time: 20 minutes +
3 hours chilling
Serves 8

200 ml (7 fl oz) double cream
300 g (10½ oz) milk chocolate,
broken into pieces
30 g (1 oz) butter
30 g (1 oz) ground hazelnuts
1 sweet pastry case (see
pages 8–9), baked blind
30 g (1 oz) whole hazelnuts

In a saucepan, bring the cream to the boil then pour over the chocolate and mix to a smooth glossy consistency. Add the butter and stir until completely melted in.

Sprinkle the ground hazelnuts over the bottom of the pastry case then pour over the chocolate ganache and spread with a palette knife.

Crush the whole hazelnuts with a rolling pin and sprinkle over the tart.

Leave to chill in the fridge for at least 3 hours before serving.

Ricotta and raspberry tart

Preparation time: 20 minutes
Cooking time: 25 minutes
Serves 8

2 eggs, separated
250 g (8¾ oz) ricotta
50 ml (2 fl oz) single cream
100 g (3½ oz) caster sugar
1 teaspoon vanilla extract
1 tablespoon cornflour
100 g (3½ oz) raspberries
1 sweet pastry case (see
   pages 8–9), baked blind

Preheat the oven to 160°C (fan oven 140°C), Gas Mark 3.

Mix the egg yolks with the ricotta, cream, sugar and vanilla extract. Once smooth, add the cornflour and mix well again.

Whisk the egg whites to firm peaks then carefully fold into the ricotta mixture.

Place the raspberries in the pastry case then pour in the ricotta mixture. Cook for 25 minutes.

Serve at room temperature or chill for a few hours.

Grape, apple and gingerbread tart

Preparation time: 30 minutes
Cooking time: 30 minutes
Serves 8

2 eggs
50 g (1¾ oz) caster sugar
250 ml (9 fl oz) thick double cream
50 g (1¾ oz) plain flour
200 g (7 oz) apples, peeled,
   cored and chopped
50 g (1¾ oz) black grapes
1 sweet pastry case (see
   pages 8–9), baked blind
1 slice gingerbread, broken
   into small pieces

Preheat the oven to 160°C (fan oven 140°C), Gas Mark 3.

Whisk the eggs and sugar together then beat in the cream and flour.

Place the fruit in the bottom of the prepared pastry case.

Pour the cream mixture over the fruit and sprinkle with the pieces of gingerbread, pressing them into the cream so that they do not burn during cooking. Cook for 30 minutes.

Pineapple, mint and coconut tart

Preparation time: 40 minutes +
12 hours chilling
Serves 8

200 g (7 oz) pineapple, peeled,
cored and cut into small pieces
a bunch of fresh mint, half kept
together and half chopped
1 sweet pastry case (see
pages 8–9), baked blind

Coconut cream
1 egg, beaten
1 egg yolk, beaten
1 tablespoon plain flour
60 g (2 oz) caster sugar
250 ml (9 fl oz) coconut milk

Place the pineapple in a pan and cook
to a compote. At the end of cooking,
add the half bunch of whole mint.
Remove the mint once the compote
has cooled. Set aside.

For the coconut cream, beat the egg,
egg yolk and flour together. Heat the
sugar and coconut milk then pour the
warm mixture into the eggs and flour,
whisking to make a smooth, thick,
glossy cream. Chill for at least
12 hours.

Spread the coconut cream over the
bottom of the pastry case and top
with the pineapple compote. Sprinkle
with the remaining chopped mint and
serve cold.

Variation: You could make this with
almond paste sides (as in the recipe
on page 48) to make it more
sophisticated (see photo opposite).

Pear and saffron semolina tart

Preparation time: 30 minutes
Cooking time: 20 minutes
Serves 8

250 ml (9 fl oz) milk
100 g (3½ oz) caster sugar
a pinch of powdered saffron
50 ml (2 fl oz) olive oil
80 g (2¾ oz) semolina
1 egg, beaten
1 sweet pastry case (see
    pages 8–9), baked blind
1 large pear, peeled, cored
    and sliced
20 g (¾ oz) sesame seeds,
    toasted

Preheat the oven to 160°C (fan oven 140°C), Gas Mark 3.

Heat the milk with the sugar, saffron and oil. When the milk is on the point of boiling, add the semolina and cook over a low heat for 3–5 minutes, stirring constantly.

Away from the heat, mix in the egg, then pour the mixture into the pastry case.

Place the pear slices in the semolina. Sprinkle with the toasted sesame seeds and cook for 20 minutes.

Serve warm or cold.

Blancmange with sesame, kiwi and strawberry

Preparation time: 20 minutes + cooling

Serves 8

2 gelatine sheets
140 g (5 oz) caster sugar
25 g (1 oz) tahini
65 ml (2 fl oz) full fat milk
250 ml (9 fl oz) double cream
1 sweet pastry case (see pages 8–9), baked blind
1 kiwi fruit, sliced
100 g (3½ oz) strawberries, sliced

Soak the gelatine in a small bowl of cold water.

In a saucepan, stir the sugar, tahini and milk over a low heat until the sugar has dissolved. Turn off the heat and add the drained gelatine. Mix well then leave to cool.

As the mixture begins to set, whip the cream until firm then fold into the sesame mixture.

Pour the cream into the pastry case and arrange the fruit on the top.

Serve cold.

Dime bar tart

Preparation time: 40 minutes +
1 hour chilling
Serves 8

120 g (4¼ oz) caster sugar
4 egg yolks
20 g (¾ oz) cornflour
½ vanilla pod
400 ml (14 fl oz) milk
200 ml (7 fl oz) double cream
a pinch of salt
1½ tablespoons butter, cut
into small pieces
1 sweet pastry case (see
pages 8–9), baked blind

Topping
250 ml (9 fl oz) double cream
30 g (1 oz) caster sugar
30 g (1 oz) Dime bars

In a bowl, mix half the sugar, the egg yolks and cornflour together. Set aside.

Add the remaining sugar, vanilla pod and its seeds, scraped out, and 60 ml (2 fl oz) of water to a saucepan. Melt the sugar over a high heat until it becomes golden, around 5 minutes.

Meanwhile, warm the milk and cream together. Remove the sugar solution from the heat and gradually add the cream mixture (watch out for lumps). Return the saucepan to the heat and bring to the boil then take off the heat again.

Away from the heat, add a third of the caramel to the egg yolk mixture, whisking thoroughly. Add this back into the remaining caramel and return to the heat. Whisk continually to thicken then remove from the heat and add the salt and butter.

Pour the caramel cream into the pastry case and leave to cool in the fridge for at least 1 hour.

Once the caramel cream is cool, whip the double cream, blend in the sugar then spread the cream onto the tart. Break the Dime bars into pieces with a rolling pin then sprinkle over the cream on the tart. Serve cold.

Apple crumble tart

Preparation time: 30 minutes +
  1 hour chilling
Cooking time: 30 minutes
Serves 8

100 g (3½ oz) chilled butter,
  cut into pieces
100 g (3½ oz) plain flour
100 g (3½ oz) roughly ground
  hazelnuts
50 g (1¾ oz) caster sugar
50 g (1¾ oz) muscovado sugar
a pinch of salt
450 g (1 lb) apples, peeled,
  cored and chopped
1 vanilla pod or 1 teaspoon
  ground cinnamon (optional)
1 sweet pastry case (see
  pages 8–9), baked blind

Make the crumble by mixing together
the butter, flour, hazelnuts, caster
sugar, muscovado sugar and salt.
Mix to a ball without overworking
the ingredients. Leave to chill in
the fridge for at least 1 hour.

Preheat the oven to 160°C (fan oven
140°C), Gas Mark 3.

Grate the crumble ball with a large-
holed grater and place the crumbs on
a baking tray. Cook for 15 minutes.

Soften the apples over a low heat
with a little water. Add the cinnamon
or seeds from the vanilla pod or leave
unflavoured as you prefer.

Place the apple in the pastry case
and cook for 15 minutes.

Once cooked, sprinkle the crumble
over the tart and serve warm or cold.

Fig and almond tart

Preparation time: 30 minutes
Cooking time: 30 minutes
Serves 8

60 g (2 oz) butter, softened
60 g (2 oz) caster sugar
1 egg
60 g (2 oz) ground almonds
1 sweet pastry case (see
   pages 8–9), baked blind
10 figs, quartered
20 g (¾ oz) flaked almonds

Preheat the oven to 160°C (fan oven 140°C), Gas Mark 3.

Prepare the almond cream by whisking the butter and sugar together until they turn pale. Whisk in the egg and ground almonds.

Using a piping bag, pipe the almond cream into the pastry case.

Space the figs in the almond cream. Fill in any gaps with any spare almond cream and sprinkle with the flaked almonds. Cook for 30 minutes and serve warm.

Housewife's apple tart

Preparation time: 30 minutes
Cooking time: 25 minutes
Serves 8

60 g (2 oz) ground almonds
60 g (2 oz) caster sugar
3 eggs
60 g (2 oz) melted butter
1 tablespoon rum
1 sweet pastry case (see
  pages 8–9), baked blind

Caramelised apple
1 apple, peeled, cored and
  quartered
1 tablespoon butter
2 tablespoons sugar

Preheat the oven to 160°C (fan oven 140°C), Gas Mark 3.

Heat the ground almonds, sugar and eggs in a bowl over a pan of simmering water. Do not allow them to boil. Once the mixture is hot, add the melted butter then the rum. Mix well to a smooth paste and pour into the pastry case.

Cut each apple quarter into two. Heat the butter and sugar in a pan then add the apple pieces and cook until caramelised.

Arrange the caramelised apple around the top of the tart and cook for 25 minutes.

Serve warm or cold.

Index

Conversion tables

The tables below are only approximate and are meant to be used as a guide only.

Approximate American/ European conversions

	USA	Metric	Imperial
brown sugar	1 cup	170 g	6 oz
butter	1 stick	115 g	4 oz
butter/ margarine/ lard	1 cup	225 g	8 oz
caster and granulated sugar	2 level tablespoons	30 g	1 oz
caster and granulated sugar	1 cup	225 g	8 oz
currants	1 cup	140 g	5 oz
flour	1 cup	140 g	5 oz
golden syrup	1 cup	350 g	12 oz
ground almonds	1 cup	115 g	4 oz
sultanas/ raisins	1 cup	200 g	7 oz

Approximate American/ European conversions

American	European
1 teaspoon	1 teaspoon/ 5 ml
½ fl oz	1 tablespoon/ ½ fl oz/ 15 ml
¼ cup	4 tablespoons/ 2 fl oz/ 50 ml
½ cup plus 2 tablespoons	¼ pint/ 5 fl oz/ 150 ml
1¼ cups	½ pint/ 10 fl oz/ 300 ml
1 pint/ 16 fl oz	1 pint/ 20 fl oz/ 600 ml
2½ pints (5 cups)	1.2 litres/ 2 pints
10 pints	4.5 litres/ 8 pints

Liquid measures

Imperial	ml	fl oz
1 teaspoon	5	
2 tablespoons	30	
4 tablespoons	60	
¼ pint/ 1 gill	150	5
⅓ pint	200	7
½ pint	300	10
¾ pint	425	15
1 pint	600	20
1¾ pints	1000 (1 litre)	35

Oven temperatures

American	Celsius	Fahrenheit	Gas Mark
Cool	130	250	½
Very slow	140	275	1
Slow	150	300	2
Moderate	160	320	3
Moderate	180	350	4
Moderately hot	190	375	5
Fairly hot	200	400	6
Hot	220	425	7
Very hot	230	450	8
Extremely hot	240	475	9

Other useful measurements

Measurement	Metric	Imperial
1 American cup	225 ml	8 fl oz
1 egg, size 3	50 ml	2 fl oz
1 egg white	30 ml	1 fl oz
1 rounded tablespoon flour	30 g	1 oz
1 rounded tablespoon cornflour	30 g	1 oz
1 rounded tablespoon caster sugar	30 g	1 oz
2 level teaspoons gelatine	10 g	¼ oz

LIBRARY
NSCC, AKERLEY CAMPUS
21 WOODLAWN RD.
DARTMOUTH, NS B2W 2R7 CANADA

DATE DUE

NOV 0 6 2014			